REDEEMED BY THE BLOOD

REDEEMED BY THE BLOOD

LOUISE RUSHING

XULON PRESS

Xulon Press
2301 Lucien Way #415
Maitland, FL 32751
407.339.4217
www.xulonpress.com

Paperback ISBN-13: 978-1-66282-265-0
Ebook ISBN-13: 978-1-66282-266-7

Dedication

I would like to dedicate *Redeemed by The Blood* to my Lord and Savior Jesus Christ. You have been so good to me. You are the lover of my soul and the lifter of my head. May this book open the eyes and hearts of every reader and bring glory to your name.

Acknowledgements

To my friend, Michelle, of 20 years

You have continuously motivated and pushed me to be my best self, stand in my truth, and tell my story.

To my daughter, Tyiesha, and my son, Charles,

You have been instrumental in my growth as a mother and grandmother. You've both taught me so much and love the real me, flaws and all.

Thank you for blessing me with three beautiful grandsons: Sar'Rae, Kjuan, and Jaden. They bring so much love, laughter, and light into my life.

To my very special friend, Sisay,

You have provided nothing but support and encouragement on my journey of self-reflection. You've helped me to love and embrace the best part of me.

To Chip Baldwin,

One of my dearest friends, not only that but family. You've always been there to encourage me and lift me up.

And to Mary Phillips-Bowen,

My friend who has shown me so much love, spoke life into me, but most importantly believed in me.

Table of Contents

Introduction

For many years, I've carried unforgiveness in my heart. Along with that came the heavy burdens which often accompany it—bitterness and anger. Oh, how these burdens weighed on my soul. There was a time when I couldn't even look myself in the mirror. I hated who I had become. I was so ashamed and yet I felt helpless. There seemed to be no hope for me to change. But then Jesus entered my life. He met me halfway and changed my life forever—praise God!

This is the story of how my life was redeemed by God's grace. How he took me, someone so ashamed I couldn't look in the mirror, and made me a brand-new creature in Christ. It did not mean that I would get things right all the time or that I would now be perfect. It meant that I was covered, redeemed by His blood and able to walk in a new life of freedom. Praise God!

Chapter 1

What is Love?

When I got married on June 16, 1990, I think I believed I was in love. Looking back, I can see that I really didn't know what love was. I had been raped by my uncle repetitively at a very young age. Anyone who has ever experienced sexual abuse can tell you it taints your perspective of love, even more so when the abuse is done by a family member. There is so much guilt and shame involved with this kind of experience that it seems almost natural to jump at any opportunity to be "loved" or wanted by somebody.

I first met my husband in 1989. We were working in a potato field in Louisiana. It was the fall harvest. He was throwing the potatoes onto the trailer and I was one of the people catching them. He tried talking to me but I acted like I didn't like him. I remember he told me I would be his wife one day but I just rolled my eyes and said, "Yeah right."

But when he asked to move in with me, I didn't even hesitate. My own insecurities had blinded me. I had been used and abused so much during my younger years that I no longer saw value in the reflection I saw in the mirror. That woman was dumb, fat, and ugly; no man wanted that women. Those are the lies I would tell my reflection and the lies that became my truth. It wasn't just the sexual abuse that brought me to this place, there was the physical and verbal abuse which I experienced at home as well.

I grew up in the South, one of ten children. There was so much anger and pain in our house. I thought this was normal growing up but I can see now how much my parents were hurting. They took that hurt out on each other and their children. Both of them drank, I suppose it was their attempt to soothe the pain inside. The curses my mama spoke over me were what established all those lies I saw every time I looked in the mirror.

It's so sad how words can smudge up that reflection in the mirror to where we no longer see the person God created us to be. That is where I had found myself. No self-worth, no value. The physical and mental abuse I had endured at home caused me to build a defensive wall around myself. It was meant to keep the world out so I would no longer be harmed however it also kept the fear locked in. Fear of being alone, abandoned, unloved.

Because of all these fears in my heart, when he asked me to marry him, I considered myself lucky that a man would even be interested in me—damaged merchandise. This marriage proposal seemed to be a lucky break; I might not get another chance at marriage. That is how little I thought of myself.

I wanted to be loved so badly but I had no real knowledge of what love was. I could feel the hole in my heart but I had no idea God was the only one who could fill it. I turned to everything I could –drinking, smoking, sex. When you find yourself in a place with that much desperation, you'll find yourself doing everything and anything just to feel something.

This relationship turned abusive even as we were dating but I continued to stay and decided to marry him. I honestly thought I could not do any better. Even though he was a licensed minister I never saw him as one because he was not living his life to please God. He was doing as he pleased. He continuously degraded me and beat me throughout our marriage but I continued to stay. I didn't have an education and I had no idea how I would support myself and my children. We moved to Seattle in 1996 and the same abuse continued. He was cheating on me and beating me. I don't say this to speak ill of him because I have since forgiven him. I say this so you will understand just how little my self-esteem was. I thought I could not do any better, I thought this would be my life from now on. There were no other options. This is when bitterness and pain began to build up inside of me along with anger and regret.

Now that I am older, I can see this was a pattern with my family—a generational curse. My parents had been hurt and abused by their parents, they brought the same kind of hurt and abuse on their children. They were broken, empty, trying to find something to fill the hole in their hearts and they turned to everything the world had to offer. Here I was doing the exact same thing. I had seen my mother abused by my father many times. It was actually a common thing to find them fighting on the front lawn. My father would tear her clothes until she was almost half naked. Here I was allowing myself to be degraded just as my mother had allowed herself to be.

I had so many issues with school because I was known for being from "that" family. I always had raggedy clothes and my parents were always fighting on the lawn. It was embarrassing. I was always told I was dumb. I wasn't good enough and it showed when I flunked two grades. After that they continued to pass me through grades but I didn't like school. I didn't think the constant teasing from other kids so often times I would play hooky, sneak down to the empty boxcars and drink.

Here I was allowing the same kind of lifestyle to play out in my own life and the lives of my children. I could clearly see how my future would play out by reflecting on my past. So, in 1999 I did something I never thought I would have the courage to do. Through the grace of God, I broke free from that curse—of abuse and dysfunction—not only for myself but for my children. I called the police and filed charges against my husband. He went to jail for two years and we got a divorce during that time.

My children would not have to be plagued by this same burden. They could be free to know what real love was between a man and woman; what true love was between God and His child. It was only through the grace of God that I was able to come out of that situation as more than just a survivor.

Chapter 2

Lack of Worth

There are many harmful things people do when they find no value in themselves. I did not see myself as beautiful or worthy so when a man would make me feel that way, I would do whatever pleased him. Morals and standards are not something you feel empowered to enforce when you have no self-worth. When you see yourself as nothing and someone shows interest, even if it is only for your body, you comply. And that is what I did over and over. Remember when I said that I didn't really know what love was? I truly didn't; not from others and certainly not for myself.

As I mentioned in the last chapter, I had built walls to protect myself from all the hurtful things my mama would speak over me. When I got out of my abusive marriage, I had constructed some new walls. Although I am a woman of color, I had decided I would never be with a man of color again. I had decided I wanted a white man. For nineteen years, I didn't even want to look at men of color or be looked at by them. The wall I had built was allowing bitterness and anger to accumulate inside of me. My husband had hurt me but rather than allowing God to heal my heart I blocked all men of color from my life in an attempt to heal myself. Oh, how foolish we can be sometimes. The Lord wants us healed; He wants us whole yet often times we make such a mess of things as we try to heal ourselves instead of allowing God to do so.

In 2017, I met a man whom I thought I loved but once again I had not yet truly learned what real love was. It had been over 17 years since I had been in a relationship. I had already committed to myself that I would not have sex outside of marriage. This was something I believed all men were after—sex—so I suppose that is why I avoided relationships altogether. That and the abuse I had suffered in my marriage. But God had allowed me to move into this brand-new building, everything was new and beautiful in this building and I was so blessed to be staying in such a place. I felt like he had given me a fresh start.

Then, one day, as I was sitting in the computer room of the building this tall handsome guy came into the room and sat down next to me. Next thing I knew, we began talking about the goodness of God. When we finished talking, I left the computer room and didn't think too much about it. Then, I saw him again in the computer room. I began talking to him about my book *All Things Have Become New* and I decided to give him a copy to read. When he was finished with it, he brought it back to me in a bag. Inside the bag was a note with his phone number and apartment number. At first, I didn't like the idea of him giving me his phone number and apartment number so I told myself I wouldn't call him. But then we had a Valentine's Day party at our building and I saw him there. He called me over to his table and asked me to sit with him.

After the party he asked if I wanted to play bingo. I said yes and so did the other people at our table so we all met for bingo at seven that night. As we began playing bingo, I began to notice this gentleman's hands. To me, they were so beautiful. I couldn't understand what was happening to me, it was as if I had been bite by a love bug. Why were his hands looking so beautiful?

I could not ignore this. And this overwhelming feeling settled over me. There was something special about this guy. For some reason, I couldn't turn it off this feeling. I started thinking about him day and night. Shortly after, we became friends. But in my mind, we were meant to be more than friends.

At first, I decided not to tell him how I felt. Instead, I kept up this best friend game. But over time the feelings that I had for him kept getting stronger and stronger until one day I told I could no longer keep them to myself. I decided it was finally time to tell him how I felt. He told me he was very flattered about the way I felt but added that he was very sorry because he did not see me in that way. He only saw us as friends.

Oh, he might as well have stabbed my heart. It was such a devasting blow to hear him say that. I felt so disappointed. I couldn't believe what I was hearing him say to me. Thankfully, with God's help, I was able to get over him. But then it happened again in 2018.

I was sitting in the lobby of my apartment building when this man, of color, came in, turned around, and looked at me with a smile. I felt offended that he was smiling at me because of the walls I had built toward men of color. I said to myself, "I know this man is not looking at me and smiling."

Little did I knew all of that was about to change. At first, we began to talk about different things one after another. I loved talking to him. He was always encouraging me, saying nice things to me and would always compliment how I was dressed. I would hang out in the lobby quite often just to catch him while he was making deliveries.

He would tell me that I was a good, smart woman. In all my life, I never had a man tell me those kinds of things. The more I saw him the more I liked him. I would think about him all the time. Whenever we saw each other, we would both get big smiles on our faces. I could feel my vow to never again fall in love with a man of color fading. I wasn't sure how this could be but it was true. I was falling in love with Peter.

When I finally got the courage to tell him I had feelings for him, he told me he felt the same. He said, "The first time I walked in and saw you sitting down in that chair I liked you. I thought you were beautiful."

Oh my God, hearing him say this made me so happy. Every time he came to deliver packages, I got this good rush all over me. Every time I saw him my heart opened more and more. I felt myself longing to be with him, to be around him. Things began to grow between us, we would talk, hug, kiss but no sex. We'd just have fun together and enjoy spending time with each other. We'd hang out in the lobby and sometimes he would come up to my apartment. But for whatever reason, whenever he said he was going to take me out something would always come up. I'd get all dressed up and ready to go but he'd never show up and when I asked him what had happened, he would always have an excuse.

For two years this went on but I never thought too much about it.

As I look back at my life from where I am now, I can see how broken and hurt I was. I ignored him not taking me out because I craved attention. During this time, I kept saying to myself maybe if I keep on being better, he'll come around but he never came around.

In his own way, he was trying to tell me that things weren't going to work out between the two of us but he never came out and said those words. Instead, he would tell me, "You're too good, you deserve better. I don't want to hurt you."

I'm not sure what he was dealing with regarding his own self-esteem but these words should have shown me we both had things we needed to deal with. I kept thinking that one day Peter would stop thinking that way. One day, he was going to realize that we should be together but that never happened. Here he was saying, "Move on, I'm not ready for this." But I continued to pursue it until I got burnt.

> ***"...but each person is tempted when they are dragged away by their own evil desire and enticed. Then, after desire has conceived, it gives birth to sin; and sin, when it is full-grown, gives birth to death." James 1: 14-15 NIV***

I wanted so badly to be loved and accepted by a man once again that I decided to take matters into my own hands. On July 14, 2020, I gave in and had sex with Peter. I suppose I believed this would change things between us for the better but all it did was leave me devasted. Not only as a woman but as a woman of God. I had failed God. I talked to Peter about it but he didn't feel the same way. He wasn't interested in a relationship.

That is when I said some things that I'm not at all proud of. But you must know them 1) because they are true and 2) because even when you are saved you make mistakes that you regret. I told him that karma would get him for his actions. I also said I would tell people the kind of man he was. I never had any intentions of reporting him, I had consented to everything. But now that it had happened, I was hurt and so I said things I didn't mean. After I told him these things, he stopped delivering to my building. I was so devasted. Not only had I had sex when I had vowed I wouldn't but I had now hurt someone as well.

But this is what we do when we lack self-worth. We pursue selfish actions to fill the hole in our hearts, this leads to sin and death. We feel even more alone and empty inside after the matter. This wasn't the first time in my life that I had allowed my lack of self-worth to provoke ungodly behavior.

When I was younger, I used to do something they now call "binge and purge". I would eat until I was so full I couldn't move, after which I would drink a lot of water and force myself to throw up. Of course, I would soon be hungry again so I'd find myself repeating this process three or four times a day.

This destructive lifestyle not only took its toll on me but produced repercussions for my children as well. In 1991, I went through my first pregnancy, never telling the doctor I had an eating disorder. My daughter was born prematurely on October 19,1991 weighing only 4lbs. 10ozs.

Despite this event, I continued on with my destructive lifestyle. It wasn't until I became pregnant with my second child that I finally stopped binging and purging. There was this one day I had put my finger down in my throat to throw up and almost choked myself to death. It was the last time I put my finger down my throat.

When we see no value in ourselves it is like walking under a giant cloud of gloom. It feels as if things will always be dark and there is no hope for seeing the sunshine ever again. For me, this feeling of despair only increased as relationships came to an end. It never matters in our eyes if the ending of a relationship is a good thing. Usually, we only focus on the fact that we are losing something.

It is important for us to realize that God cannot hand us what he needs to hand us if our hands are already full. There are things that we have to let go of in life. King Solomon said for everything there is a season; this is true even for relationships.

"To everything there is a season, A time for every purpose under heaven:" Ecclesiastes 3:1

Sometimes, with relationships, though we are unable to see the light at the end of the tunnel until we've stepped away. Sometimes we are too close to see that letting go will be a good thing in the end.

> ***"A time to gain, and a time to lose; a time to keep, and a time to throw away;" Ecclesiastes 3: 6***

Losing relationships did not seem like a good thing to me. It was always painful. However, through the pain, God was able to open my eyes to the truth. I did not need the love of others to fill the hole in my heart, His love was more than enough for me. I needed to accept that He was truly all I needed. I also had to learn to appreciate the person God made me to be.

Looking back, I can see all the times I tried pursuing men when I should have been pursuing God. There He was pursuing me, never turning His back on me. I can see clearly the many times in my life when God was loving on me yet I continued to push him away.

I'm so sorry, God, for treating you that way. Thank you for forgiving me.

It took me a while to learn this lesson but I finally understand God wants me to appreciate myself. To see value in myself as part of His creation. Recently, with this truth, I made up my mind to start working out in the pool in an effort to care for myself. I have been doing it for over two years now. I'm losing weight, my blood pressure is stable, my heart rate is good, and I can move around good. God wants us to care for His creation, I think that too often we forget that includes caring for ourselves as well.

Chapter 3

To Think is To Do

Although I was devasted regarding what had happened between me and Peter I am so thankful God allowed this situation to open my eyes. I have not seen Peter since the day I said all those hurtful things to him. However, if I am ever able to see him again, I will apologize and ask for forgiveness. I never should have said the things that I told him. I thank God for him, because of him God was able to open my eyes to many things I had not admit to myself. Many areas that I had not allowed God to deal with.

See, when I gave in and had sex with Peter, this was something that I had allowed to build up in my life for over 17 years. For nine years, my husband cheated on me, beat me and called me all kind of names. It was humiliated to know that he was out with other women. So, eventually, I convinced myself that I could have any man I wanted to—in my mind—without ever being hurt again. For many years I was having sex with men in my mind because I thought that I would never be with anybody. Because of the pain, I wasn't sure that I wanted to physically be with a man again but that didn't stop me from having sex with whatever man I wanted to in my mind. This was a lie from the enemy, and it set me on this path of failure.

I know this because in Matthew 5: 27-28 Jesus said, ***"You have heard that it was said to those of old, 'You shall not commit adultery.' But I say to you that whoever looks at a woman to lust for her has already committed adultery with her in his heart."***

I had given Peter such a bad time for having sex with me that day but after we parted ways God brought me down off my pedestal and showed me the error of my ways. I had chastised Peter for one event but here I was doing this for many years now. I had no idea of the damage I was causing in my mind or the pain I was setting myself up to experience. I thank God for freeing me of that spirit of deception and lust. Through this experience, I learned to let Jesus be the man of my life. He is the only man who truly loves me unconditionally. I know I am made in his image, in his likeness. I do not have to pursue affection from men because he already has so much for me.

Because of his grace and through his mercy, I have learned to love and respect who I am. My self-worth is more precious than diamonds. I have a God who loves me. Knowing this has allowed me to not be ashamed or afraid to look in the mirror. I know I've been washed in the blood of Jesus Christ.

The Lord has shown me how unstable I've been. I degraded myself and it all started in my mind. I believed that I was ugly and unattractive. Then I allowed myself to pursue sin, in my mind. Everything was happening in my mind. I needed to give my mind over to God. Allow him to cleanse it, free me from these awful thoughts and lies. A lot of these lies in my mind had been placed there by myself but there were also some placed by other people—my ex-husband, my father, my mother, kids at school.

"For though we walk in the flesh, we do not war according to the flesh. For the weapons of our warfare are not carnal but mighty in God for pulling down strongholds, casting down arguments and every high thing that exalts itself against the knowledge of God, bringing every thought into captivity to the obedience of Christ, and being ready to punish all disobedience when your obedience is fulfilled." 2 Corinthians 10:3-6

As Christians, we are at war every day but not against the things we can see. Our mind is constantly under attack by Satan. That is why it is so important for us to take every thought captive. We cannot let non-productive ideas wander through our mind. Negativity towards ourselves or others needs to be stamped out. Thoughts of lust or envy need to be dealt with immediately. The longer these thoughts are allowed to linger they more comfortable we become with them. And when we become comfortable with sinful thoughts we sin!

With this knowledge we must ask ourselves, is it worth it? One tiny thought can lead to so much destruction and devastation when we don't turn it over to God.

"Finally, brethren, whatever things are true, whatever things are noble, whatever things are just, whatever things are pure, whatever things are lovely, whatever things are of good report, if there is any virtue and if there is anything praiseworthy—meditate on these things. The things which you learned and received and heard and saw in me, these do, and the God of peace will be with you." Philippians 4:8-9

I share this with you so that you can truly see the love of God. I am a Christian yet I sinned. It is just as the Apostle Paul says in Romans,

> ***"We know that the law is spiritual; but I am unspiritual, sold as a slave to sin. I do not understand what I do. For what I want to do I do not do, but what I hate I do. And if I do what I do not want to do, I agree that the law is good. As it is, it is no longer I myself who do it, but it is sin living in me. For I know that good itself does not dwell in me, that is, in my sinful nature. For I have the desire to do what is good, but I cannot carry it out. For I do not do the good I want to do, but the evil I do not want to do—this I keep on doing. Now if I do what I do not want to do, it is no longer I who do it, but it is sin living in me that does it." Romans 7:14-20***

I want to do the right things but here I am doing the very thing I know is wrong. This is why it is so important to continue to seek God. Our hearts will deceive us. They will lead us down the wrong path if we allow them to take the driver's seat. But the Holy Spirit will never mislead us. The Holy Spirit is always there to direct us down the right path. I knew having sex that day would not be the right thing to do. However, I had allowed the thought to linger in my mind so much that it seemed like the only option.

> ***"Finally, brothers and sisters, whatever is true, whatever is noble, whatever is right, whatever is pure, whatever is lovely, whatever is admirable—if anything is excellent or praiseworthy—think about such things. Whatever***

you have learned or received or heard from me, or seen in me—put it into practice. And the God of peace will be with you." Philippians 4:8-9

When we allow ourselves to think on things that are not inline with God we set ourselves up to fail, we set ourselves up to sin. That is why we are told over and over to choose between God and the world. We can choose God and His ways, or we can choose the ways of the world. But we cannot have both!

Chapter 4

Forgiveness

A lot of my issues with men came from the examples, of lack of examples, I was given in my life. I did not see a healthy relationship between my father and mother. I've already told you about the fights on the front lawn. There was abuse inside the house as well. Then there was the sexual abuse from my uncle which painted a tainted picture of what men thought of women. And of course, my ex-husband did not add anything good to these examples. He only caused me to have even more distrust in men.

Throughout life, it seems we often gather up issues as we move along. Issues with trust, confidence, fears, self-esteem, and many other things. A good portion of our issues often develop because of the actions of other people. I have mentioned a lot of my issues with self-esteem stem from how my mother treated me. It is okay for us to recognize when people have caused us pain. We have to get to the root of things in order to pull up the issue entirely and allow God to bring us total healing.

However, when identifying where the pain entered our life we then are faced with a crossroads—blame or forgiveness.

Blaming those who caused us pain will only cause further pain. There is a saying, "Hurt people, hurt people." This is true. I know that my mother and father had a lot of pain in their lives, they then turned around and hurt me along with my siblings as well as each other. But I cannot dwell on the pain that they caused me. The only thing this will accomplish is causing more pain. Instead, I have to let it go, I have to forgive. Unforgiveness is like a cancer, it could be the death of you. It will slowly eat away at you until you find yourself robbed of every ounce of joy and peace God had for you.

Forgiveness is the best form of love. It takes a strong person to say sorry and an even stronger person to forgive. When we forgive someone, we are relinquishing our desire for them to owe us. When someone has caused us pain, we typically think they owe us. We deserve to be treated better; this debt must be repaid. But when we forgive them, we cancel their debt against us.

"And whenever you stand praying, if you have anything against anyone, forgive him, that your Father in heaven may also forgive you your trespasses." Mark 11:25

God takes forgiveness very seriously. He didn't send His only Son, Jesus Christ, to redeem us from our sins because he had to. God sent Jesus to provide the forgiveness for our sins because he wanted to. We should view forgiveness in the same way. Forgiveness is good for our hearts. The other person may not accept our forgiveness, they may not appreciate that we have forgiven them but that is ok. It is more for our hearts.

Unforgiveness only plants seeds of anger, bitterness, and discontentment in our hearts. Forgiveness is not something we do for other people, we do it for ourselves to get well and move on in our life. We need to forgive those who insult, attack, belittle, or take us for granted. But more than that, we need to forgive ourselves for allowing them to hurt us. For allowing their opinion and actions to affect how we see ourselves.

The greatest gift my Heavenly Father has given me has been to teach me how to forgive. He showed me how to truly forgive my mama, daddy, husband and all kinds of other people who have hurt me both physically and emotionally. I can now look at them with forgiveness in my heart.

I can look at my ex-husband and through eyes of forgiveness I see him as a brother. I no longer see the abuse and pain. The same can be said of my mother. I spoke about this in my first book, *All Things Have Become New*. When God broke the bitterness off my heart, I was able to see my mother as God saw her, hurting and broken. Then I was able to show her love and kindness.

I hope that you are able to truly understand what I am saying here. If you don't forgive, it will destroy you just like cancer. We need God's forgiveness and others need our forgiveness.

> ***"And be kind to one another, tenderhearted, forgiving one another, even as God in Christ forgave you." Ephesians 4:32***

Chapter 5

Pastor Sisay

When you've been abused in any way—by a friend, spouse, family member—you'll often times put up a wall to protect yourself from further pain. I have spoken about this a few times now. It happened when I put a wall up against hurtful words and when I decided to build a wall against having relationships with men of color. A lot of the time these walls can be installed without our direct knowledge. If a friend betrays your trust, you're not quick to trust others. If a spouse treats you horrible, you're quick to think all men will treat you the same. This comes more as a defensive response than a conscious decision that is made.

On July 28, 2020, only a few short day after the incident with Peter, I met someone that shook one of my walls once again. (I'm thankful God is all about tearing down our walls!) This wall-shaker was a wonderful Ethiopian man named Sisay.

I had an appointment with the doctor and that's where I crossed paths with Sisay. He was polite and nice; he treated me with so much respect and kindness during that ride. I had never experienced that from a man before. We talked about the differences in our cultures and different foods. Talking to him just made me feel so good.

When we parted ways that day, he gave me his phone number and told me to call him sometime. He told me we could go out for coffee and get to know each other. I couldn't believe this was happening to me. He had given me *his* phone number.

At this point of my life, I had been single for over 20 years. I was excited to meet such a gentleman. I had met two other men a few years back, one in 2017 and then Peter in 2018 but neither of those went anywhere. In fact, things with Peter had just ended disastrously.

I decided to call Sisay three days after the encounter. We decided to go out for dinner. It was such a wonderful time. We decided to continue spending time together.

Sisay never talked to me abusive or crazy, he didn't make excuses or beat around the bush regarding his intentions like all the men I had dated before; he touched my heart. Not only did he treat me with respect by what he said but also by what he did, or rather didn't do, he never pushed sex on me. Instead of chasing after my body he sought to know me. Yes, that's right, he wanted to have conversations and get to know me.

We began a beautiful friendship. I had never had this kind of experience with a man. I believe God put him in my life so I could experience a different kind of man. Unfortunately, because he was so different from any man I had encountered in the past, it wasn't difficult to fall in love with him. When I told him how I felt, he said he didn't feel the same.

Although he was honest with me that he was not ready to be in a relationship it still kind of hurt my heart. I very much respected his honesty and our friendship continued to bloom. He asked if I could be his spiritual mentor.

Here I was looking for what I wanted out of this relationship never once considered the obligation that I had to God. This man had gone through his own heartache and pain. He wanted to seek God with everything he had and hoped I would walk with him on this journey. And here I was having just thrown myself at a man and found myself rejected trying to thrown myself at yet another.

God was certainly trying to wake me up and show me the areas that I needed to deal with in my own heart. Even though our relationship will not be going the direction I would have liked it to go I still thank God for the opportunity to have such an amazing friend as Sisay. I pray that God will bless him with everything that he needs in his life.

I tell you about him because for me Sisay has been God's way of showing me that there are good men out there. Men who will appreciate and respect women rather than seeking their bodies. He showed me that I do not have to lay on my back to get a man's attention.

I wanted so badly to have a relationship. But through Sisay's gentle rejection God was able to show me His love for me. Here I was once again chasing after what I thought would satisfy me in my life. This was not a bad thing but even good things can turn bad if they are not what God has planned for us. I could have completely walked away from Sisay after he told me he wasn't interested in being anything more than friends but thank God I didn't!

Sisay and I are still best of friends and we are going to continue to be. I would like every woman who is reading this book, every man too, to understand that finding someone special for your life will not complete you—only God can complete us. God is the only one who can satisfy that thirst within our soul. If we try to impose this position on another human being, chances are we will both be left dissatisfied.

I know that if God desires for me to have somebody in my life, a husband, he will bring that man to me. But for the time being, it is better that I stay put on and continue to walk the platform that He has planted in my life. I thank God because everywhere I go my platform is with me.

God is the greatest He makes a way for me and so I just want to give Him glory and honor.

In Chapter 2, I spoke about losing things. We lose relationships and feel devasted for our situation, never considering that God may have better things. Sisay is a wonderful man. Not having more than a friendship with him might seem like a loss in some women's eyes. But I choose not to see this as a sad part of my story. A few months ago, Sisay told me that he had never in his life met a woman like me. Those words truly blessed my heart. I told him that I had never met a man like him. He encourages me to want to be a better version of myself. Not in a way of doubting myself but in a way of wanting to understand the person God created in me. To find that Louise and help her to grow more and more.

I am truly blessed that I am able to continue our friendship and be content as friends. I have had many struggles throughout my life and there have been a lot of lessons I learned along the way. But I do not dismiss those struggles and hard times, they are what made me who I am today. Through everything that I have gone through, God has allowed me to be content whatever my situation. Without all those hard times, I wouldn't be who I am today and I wouldn't be able to appreciate the things that my Lord and Savior brought me through. Amen, All Day Long!

Chapter 6

A New Beginning

My whole life is a new beginning all because of my Lord and Savior Jesus Christ. I will always give Him praises, honor, and glory for all that He has done. Yes, my life has been exceedingly difficult and painful at times. I've experienced many disappointments and heartaches. I've been physically and emotionally abused repeatedly but I've made it through by the grace of God.

I struggled with addiction to alcohol and cigarettes but God delivered me from those things. Because of God, my children never had to see me do these things. God delivered me from them in January 1993 when my daughter, Tyiesha, was only 14 mouth old. I'm truly grateful for this deliverance.

The spirit of fear has had an extraordinarily stronghold on my life. It kept me in bondage for many decades. Telling me I was not good enough, I was a disgrace, I deserved to be abandoned and abused. For too long, I allowed this spirit to manipulate and control me. But now I am free! Hallelujah! Fear does not hold me down because the perfect love of Jesus set me free. Fear does not control my life anymore I do not have a hopeless state of mind no more night terrors or nightmares to haunt me. I found hope in Jesus Christ He came to my rescue.

> ***"There is no fear in love; but perfect love casts out fear, because fear involves torment. But he who fears has not been made perfect in love." 1 John 4:18***

This is why I say I truly didn't know what love was until I met Jesus Christ. I lived in the torment of fear for so long then Christ came and brought be freedom and peace. I'm no longer a slave to fear, it does not direct my path. It is because of this freedom that I cannot and will not stop giving God honor and praise. He loves me More than I can ever could have imagined being loved and when he came in my life I was able to know what true love really meant.

Christ Jesus delivered me and set my soul free. He brought me out of darkness into the marvelous light. I know now what the devil meant for evil God had turned it around for my good. But even in all of this good there are still struggles that arise. I don't know if there are many people who would have survived the life I lived. Abuse, homelessness, and all the other addictions and heartaches I experienced along the way. But I know that only by God's strength was I able to survive these things.

Recently, I've been having problems with both of my ankles. When I was a little child, both of my ankles were broken but I never went to the doctor. I thought that my ankle was only sprang back then, I never suspected it was broke. So, I would climb into the attic and get old sheets that had been left in the house by previous tenants. I'd tear those sheets up and tie them around my ankles. Then I would be able to limp around despite the pain. Of course, like any problem that is not dealt with correctly, this only led to other problems further down the road.

When I got older, I started having problems with both my ankles once again. In 2010, I began having problems with my ankles once again. Walking became so painful. I went to the doctor and they decided to perform a reconstructive surgery on my left ankle. It didn't work and they ended up having to go back in and fuse the ankle. That worked. In 2016, I was able to get an ankle replacement on my right ankle. Praise God! But in 2019, I started having problems again and when I went in for another surgery, I found out that it had collapsed. I was so devastated when the doctor told me this. He gave me three options. For one of the options, they could get the equipment from Europe and rebuild my ankle or they could amputate. There was another option but these are the ones that weighed on me the most. The doctor even advised that the third option would be the best one for me. But I asked God what option I should chose and I know what He spoke to me. So, I went with the option where they would import the parts from Europe and rebuild my ankle. The surgery went well and everything is looking good.

God is so good; He has allowed me to still be able to walk despite what the doctors said. They had suggested they might need to amputate my ankle but God had other plans for me. I can see the miracle of God still working in my life.

Sometimes it is difficult to see God's hand at work. For me, this has been true when I focus on the bad things rather than keep my eyes on the Lord. Have you been there? When you fall into a pit and cry, woe is me? As Christians, there is no reason for us to live in this kind of defeat. Yes, things may get difficult throughout our life but there is never a reason to give up hope. God is faithful always and He will see us through everything.

"Are not five sparrows sold for two copper coins? And not one of them is forgotten before God. But the very hairs of

> ***your head are all numbered. Do not fear therefore; you are of more value than many sparrows." Luke 12: 6-7***

The Bible tells us God knows the number of hairs on our heads. If he knows this kind of details about us, I believe it is safe to say that He cares for all our needs and will see us through everything.

> ***"Trust in the Lord with all your heart, and lean not on your own understanding; In all your ways acknowledge Him, and He shall direct your paths. Do not be wise in your own eyes; Fear the Lord and depart from evil. It will be health to your flesh, and strength to your bones." Proverbs 3:5-8***

Chapter 7

Reap What You Sow

So many decisions I made in my life were because of what was planted inside of me as I grew up. Anger. Bitterness. Fear. I was hurt and wounded; it was hard to let go of the pain until Jesus Christ came in my life. As I mentioned before, it all started when I was very young. I didn't have a good childhood I had a bad childhood. These are the things that I was taught growing up—to drink, have sex, cuss, fight, be angry, be bitter—when destructive behaviors are planted inside of you it is only certain that you will reap destruction.

This is why King Solomon said, ***"Train up a child in the way he should go, and when he is old he will not depart from it." (Proverbs 22:11)*** Whatever ways a child learns are the ways they will live their life. I was not taught the ways of the Lord; I was taught the ways of the world.

I never thought that I would have any children but God blessed me to have two beautiful children, a daughter and a son. God is such an Amazing God! He has also blessed me with three handsome grandsons. I love them so much. I love to see all they are accomplishing in their lives.

There have been a lot of things I didn't get to do in my life like finish school. I mentioned in one of the earlier chapters how I had flunked two grades and then they pushed me through two other grades even though I didn't have the skills needed to pass those grades. It was during my school years when I began drinking. I played hooky to get away from all the awful things kids would say to me. Then, during that time I would sit in boxcars and drink. It never occurred to me during that time that I was planting seeds in my life which would reap a harvest. Because they were seeds of destruction, I was reaping destruction.

But by the grace of God, I've been able to sow new seeds and see Him do a new thing within my legacy. When I got a divorce, I had decided things would be different for my children. I would raise them for the Lord. My kids would say, "How come my friends can turn it up and party but we can't?"

I would just say, "No, we're not going to do things that way."

I wanted them to know who God was and how much He loved them. And because of the abuse I had experienced when I was growing up I did not fight my children when they decided to do things their own way and turn from God. I knew they had to figure out who God was to them in their own way. That does not mean I didn't continue to talk to them about God and the importance of having Him in their lives. Those were all seeds which were sown.

And I have been blessed to see that harvest. Both of my children graduated from high school. And we have many conversations about the Lord.

When my daughter was three years old, the Lord spoke to me about her. He said she was going to do great things in His name. When He spoke these things to me, I immediately believed him. I knew that he said, ***"So shall My word be that goes forth from My mouth; It shall not return to Me void, But it shall accomplish what I please, And it shall prosper in the thing for which I sent it." Isaiah 55:11***

There were things I had never got a chance to do in life—graduate high school, go to college—but I was claiming them for my daughter. God said she was going to do great things in His name and I believed they would come to pass.

My beautiful daughter came to me the day that she was graduating from college and said, "Mom, when you see me walk down that aisle getting my certificate remember that is you. Remember everything that you didn't get the chance to do I'm doing it for you. This is for you; ma'am and I thank you for everything you have done in my life."

When she told me that I was so happy to hear how God was blessing my family through my children. I did not have to count my lack of education as a loss because he was accomplishing great things in the lives of my children.

> ***"Therefore know that the Lord your God, He is God, the faithful God who keeps covenant and mercy for a thousand generations with those who love Him and keep His commandments;" Deuteronomy 7:9***

I'm so proud of everything my children have accomplished but most of all I am thankful they have Christ in their lives. That is fulfillment of my biggest dream of all.

Many of us go through life hoping to see the harvest spring up in our own lives or hoping to see it spring up where we planted the seeds. I could have found myself bitter of all the things I had "lost" in life but instead I took joy to see them fulfilled through my children.

> ***"And let us not grow weary while doing good, for in due season we shall reap if we do not lose heart. Therefore,***

as we have opportunity, let us do good to all, especially to those who are of the household of faith." Galatians 6:9-10

There is no point of record keeping with God. Do the tasks that you have been assigned to do—be a mother, a pastor, a singer, a wife, a friend, an artist—whatever the task God has given you do it for His glory and you will see a harvest reaped for His glory.

Chapter 8

My Savior

So much pain and suffering affected my life but God saved me. That is why I am writing this story, so that people will know whatever they are suffering through God can deliver them and heal them. This means you! He can set your soul free no matter what you're facing right now in your life. There is nothing in your life that he cannot fix He's waiting for you right now to come to him, He is right there for you. Trust Him and let him heal your broken, wounded heart. I know He can do it for you because He did it for me.

I can look in the mirror and love the woman I see. For over 20 years I wouldn't look in the mirror because when I did look all I saw was pain. When seeing my reflection, all I ever heard were the lies I had been told, "You'll never be nothing. You're too ugly, too fat. Nobody will ever love you."

I believed these lies for so many years of my life. They caused me to live such a destructive lifestyle but through the grace of God my life has been changed. I am able to look at the plant on the cover of my first book, *All Things Have Become New*, and thank God. Those leaves sprouting out of this new plant are just like my hands raised up in thankfulness to God. He made me new. I am growing into a new woman through his grace.

The old woman had to die so that the new woman could live. And here I am now, living my new life. I have struggles, trials and tribulation but through it all God is and will always continue to lead and direct me.

> ***"Come to me, all you who are weary and burdened, and I will give you rest. Take my yoke upon you and learn from me, for I am gentle and humble in heart, and you will find rest for your souls. For my yoke is easy and my burden is light." Matthew 11:28-30***

At one time in my life, I used to be a loner. I'd stay to myself and wouldn't talk to anybody. I'd keep all of my opinions to myself because I was so afraid of what others might think if I actually voiced them. Let it be known that Satan is the one who wants to silence us. God gives us a new song to sing a testimony to share with others for His glory. Satan will keep you quiet in whatever way he can. He will tell you that your words aren't worth saying, he will tell you nobody wants to hear you and if he cannot keep you quiet with those lies, he will try another approach. He will tell you that you'll look foolish or that people will turn against you.

This last one can be a difficult one because it can turn true. There may be times when people will laugh or turn against us but this will only hurt us if we are finding our worth somewhere other than God.

Satan will feed us every negative thing he can to keep our minds in bondage. Remember 'hurt people, hurt people'. Satan knows he has already been defeated so he will do everything he can to bring down God's children.

But don't let this worry you or keep you from moving forward. Remember that God loves you and he will always be there for you no matter what you face in your life.

"What then shall we say to these things? If God is for us, who can be against us?" Romans 8:31

"The thief does not come except to steal, and to kill, and to destroy. I have come that they may have life, and that they may have it more abundantly." John 10:10

"I will praise You, for I am fearfully and wonderfully made; Marvelous are Your works, And that my soul knows very well." Psalm 139:14

These words are so true to me now and forever more. I am a brand-new soul in Christ. There have been times, even on my spiritual journey, where I have struggled to believe these truths. I knew that God would never leave me or fail me but there were times I failed him and felt so discouraged, how could I carry on? Now I know that God will bring me through every situation.

On October 29, 2011, I became an ordained minister. Peoples said that I couldn't do it but God allowed me to do it. Even during the hard times, I have stayed focused on the things of God because it was him that brought me out of the darkness into the marvelous light. He made it possible for me to do this not because I am anybody special but so that people all over the world could know that he can do it for them too.

If we trust and believe in him despite what we've gone through, despite our past, He is faithful to complete his work in us.

> ***"being confident of this very thing, that He who has begun a good work in you will complete it until the day of Jesus Christ;" Philippians 1:6***

The enemy means to destroy us but if we allow God to come in, he can heal, deliver, and set us free from anything that the enemy brings against us. I am a firm believer that once we make up our minds to do something we can do it because God's word says, ***"You are of God, little children, and have overcome them, because He who is in you is greater than he who is in the world." 1 John 4:4***

I thank God for that and I thank God how I never stopped believing or trusting him no matter what. Through all the pain, hurt and humiliation that I've been through, even though I know there were times I should have been dead; God spared my life to let others know that we can make it through Him.

Chapter 9

The Perfect Christian Life

In Chapter 7, I talked about all the good things that came out of my children's lives. I lived a Christian life; I spoke to them about God and I got to see them accomplish things I didn't get to accomplish in life like finishing school and going to college.

However, I don't by any means want you to think that everything was perfect with my children. We struggled hard when they were growing up. There were moments that my kids were as bad as hell, I'm not even exaggerating, you can confirm it with them. Now, I know there were many things which contributed to this but there was a part of me that felt like it should be easier because I was trying to live my life as a Christian.

I went through a lot of physical and emotional abuse when I was growing up, as I have told you. With ten kids and no God in the mix, you know there was bound to be struggles. I suppose I shouldn't say 'no God' because whenever my mother got drunk, she would talk about God. But that was the extent of our knowledge about God. We were not given a Godly example of how to live our lives. There were all kinds of things allowed in the house—sex, alcohol, molestation. It was a bad environment.

So, as I grew up, I thought those things were normal. It was fine to smoke, fine to drink, fine to have sex with whomever wants to have sex with you. That's what I saw my parents doing so that's what I figured we were supposed to do in life. Never once did I realize this was a habit being passed down from generation to generation. What my parents do, I see and I do. Then what I do my kids will see and they will do. A pattern which will continue down through generations until someone decided to flip the script and change things up.

That is exactly what happened when I called the police on my husband. I was rewritten the script that had been written for my children and grandchildren and all future generations to come. That phone call was me saying, "Enough is enough." And I didn't even realize it! I had no idea how God would use this one step, one action to rewrite everything.

Now, that is not to say everything fell into place and was beautiful. No! If I told you that God knows I would be lying. When my kids were babies and I walked away from cigarettes and alcohol I told myself I wouldn't go back. So, I didn't allow these things in my house. After my husband went to jail and we divorced, I didn't bring any men into my house. I focused on serving God and raising my children.

And let me tell you something, raising those two was no walk in the park!

I took the kids to church but as soon as they were old enough to decide they didn't want to go to church they stopped going. I told them I wouldn't force them to go to church, it had to be their decision. Then I added, "But just because you ain't going to go doesn't mean I will stop. I'm not going to stop serving him."

Some Christian parents might hear this and think I'm wrong for not making them go but I don't understand why. God didn't force me to come to Him, why should I force my children to go to Him? When I was growing up, I was forced to do many things I didn't want to do and all it did was form bitterness and resentment in my heart that God later healed me of.

I told my children, "You don't have to go but ya'll coming back."

They'd say, "No, I don't want to be saved."

But I'd say, "Ya'll coming back."

Because I knew God's word said,

> ***"Start children off on the way they should go, and even when they are old they will not turn from it." Proverbs 22:6***

I had taken my children to church, I had taught them about God, I had lived the best example I could of following him, so now all I could do was stand on this promise. God was going to bring these children back to him.

Sadly, too many Christians focus on their image instead of God. "Oh, Lord, what are people going to think if I'm serving you and my child are hellions?"

This is also why so many people don't want to serve God, because they think every part of your life has to be perfectly put together. Well, if that's true I guess God forgot to look at some people's resumes because as I said before, the Bible is full of a bunch of imperfect people, just like this world is.

King David, Moses, Paul—you know what all of these big heroes of the Bible have in common? They all killed somebody. How's that for imperfect? No matter what we've been through God already knows and yet he still wants you! This is true for our children as well.

I shed those tears, "Oh, God, I'm trying to live a Godly life for you and my kids are out turning it out. Oh, God, what do I need to do?"

If your kids are out there turning it up, this doesn't affect you. You need to still continue to be the man or woman of God that you were called to be. You cannot control your kids actions anymore than your parents could control your actions. That isn't to say your children don't need to be disciplined and have consequences for their actions while they are living under your roof. They do! But don't allow the devil to get to you through your kids.

Instead take the advice that God gave me. I cried, "What am I going to do? I'm raising them for you and these are the things they are doing?"

God said, "Louise, what did you do when you were younger? You know you didn't have it all together. But you know what you didn't have? A praying mother. Start praying for your kids and let me handle them."

Oh, wow, what a powerful thing to hear.

I wanted to hope the best for my kids. There were moments I heard my daughter was out turning it up and I said, "No, she's not doing that I'm a Christian."

I was wrong. And it is only in the truth that we can be set free.

"Then you will know the truth, and the truth will set you free." John 8:32

God honors you more when you are truthful with yourself instead of lying. So many people are in bondage because they are afraid of the shame of what people will think. You know why I'm putting all this in the book? Because the devil has no power over me. He can't make me feel shame for anything in this book because I am redeemed by the blood. Not the things that were done to me, the things I chose to do of my own free will, or the things my children chose to do.

I cannot lie and say, "I'm a Christian and my life is perfect." I suppose I could do that but I'm not going to! Because if I did I would be lying to God too and I wouldn't be acknowledging all that he has brought me through. I'm grateful that I am able to tell you all this so that you can see God is able to do exceedingly, abundantly more than you think or ask of Him. He is God and He is able!

> ***"Now to him who is able to do immeasurably more than all we ask or imagine, according to his power that is at work within us," Ephesians 3:20***

As I thought about everything I would put out there in this book, God told me, "Baby, just release it, allow me to put my spirit in you. And when you release this, you'll be allowing other people to be released from bondage.

So, let's talk a little more about these children and how they turned out.

My son was two years old when I got separated from his dad. I'm not sure what started it but I could see over the years that bitterness and anger were continuing to build inside of him. He'd get so mad he would just tear stuff up. It grieved my soul how angry and bitter he would act towards his dad. It was something that he had decided in his heart to act upon because I never justified, the way he acted. I know some people might have told him he was right to feel that way but I couldn't do that. I wanted him to love his dad and forgive his dad. That is what God told us to do.

He got in trouble at school as well. Things got so bad that they kicked him out of school and sent him to another school for troubled kids. It wasn't until I kicked him out of the house that I finally saw him change.

See, when I was growing up I watched my mom allow my grown brother to stay with her, she would take his food to his room and wait on him. At that time of my life, I said, "Oh no, I'll never wait on my kids like that."

I was there mother, God had me in their lives to nurture them, teach them, raise them, and protect them. But the moment my kids thought they knew better was the moment I decided they could try it out. My daughter moved into an apartment when she was eighteen. I thought it was good because she made it seem like she was moving there on her own. I had no idea she was moving in with her boyfriend. She ended up getting pregnant the next year.

Then there was my son. I began to notice the same kind of habits some of my brothers and nephews were exhibiting. I didn't want my son to stay in my house and never amount to anything so one day in December 2016, I said, "Bro, you gotta go."

He said, "Where am I going to go?"

I didn't know where he was going to go but I knew it was time to get him out of my house. He was beginning to act disrespectful towards me and thought he could come and go as he pleased. If he wanted to be grown it was time for him to be grown…outside of my house. I told him that I had to have him leave because I loved him.

He, of course, was angry and said, "You're kicking me out and that's loving me?"

I think that was the hardest thing I ever had to do as a mother. He was so angry with me that we were estranged for three or four months before he finally started talking to me again. I cried and prayed so hard every day that he was gone. I knew there were times when he was staying in his car but I had to give him to God. He was God's kid before he was my child.

Things may not always happen the way we want them to happen but I can tell you that God is faithful because he heard my prayers and turned my son around. Today, my son comes to me and tells me thank you for putting me out. I let my son go and God brought him back around. Now when he wants advice, he comes to mama to get spiritual advice.

Just like I said with relationships. Sometimes we hang on to things so tightly because we are afraid to lose them but when we hand them over to God they are never lost. Releasing my son was painful but God needed me to release him so he could work on him. I wasn't going to be disrespected by my kids. I stood my ground and I trusted God. And He came through!

What if I hadn't trusted God? What if I had allowed my son to stay with me, disrespect me, and be lazy? Would he be the man that he is today? I don't believe so. This was once again a pattern that was being broken off my family and future generations to come.

Even though he had so much bitterness and anger towards his father my son now has so much respect for his dad. When he bought a new car, he gave his old car to his father.

My daughter invites me on vacations with her family and I don't have to pay for anything. Both my kids tell me, "Mom, we know it wasn't easy for you to raise us. We know we didn't make it easy."

I said, "You think?"

They tell me, "Mom, when we think of you and all you've done for us, we know we wouldn't be where we are today if it wasn't for you."

Hearing this brings joy to my heart because I know how many tears, I cried over those children during the first eighteen years of their lives. So many times, that I said, "God, what is happening with these children."

I know they will have struggles with their kids and they are going to see. But I'm grateful that we have God in the midst of everything in our life. He truly has made the differences.

And that is what I want people to know. We can't look at our children and say, "I'm a Christian why are you doing these things? Didn't I raise you right?"

God has extended us so much grace and mercy. We need to understand that our children are people too. They need some grace and mercy if we truly want them to see God. We have to live it out more than we talk about it or lecture them on it.

My kids said they never understood how come all their friends' parents allowed them to party and turn it up but I never allowed that in my house. But now that they are older, they are grateful for the standard I set for our household. They can now see I wanted a different life for them.

> ***"Do not conform to the pattern of this world, but be transformed by the renewing of your mind. Then you will be able to test and approve what God's will is—his good, pleasing and perfect will." Romans 12:2***

I had experienced the "pattern of the world" in my life as I was growing up. I saw it in the lives of family members as well. I wanted something different for my children. I believed in the power of God. I believed that he could change things—and he did! And if he can do it for me and my family, he can do it for you and yours.

You don't have to be perfect to serve Jesus, you just have to be willing. You don't need to get everything right before you start serving him, if you try to do that you're never going to serve him. You come to him just as you are and that's enough.

I made a lot of mistake on this journey and if I hadn't made them I wouldn't be who I am here today. No matter what I went through I never gave up trusting in God. I may have gone through the ringer but by trusting in God, he brought it all back to around. What the devil meant for evil, God turned it all around for good. Just like he did for others in his Word.

> ***"You intended to harm me, but God intended it for good to accomplish what is now being done, the saving of many lives." Genesis 50:20***

When Jesus died on the cross, he died for us even though we were yet still sinners. If Jesus can die on that cross and forgive us, we should be able to do that same thing for others if we have God inside of us. I thank God for this! That is why I believe God doesn't care if you are dancing on the pole or on death row, he wants you to come. You can be forgiven. God loves everybody, no matter what we have done. The only thing He can't stand is sin. That is why we as believers have to stop degrading ourselves. We have to get out from under the patterns of this world.

"Well, this is the way my family has always done it." Guess what? You better change the way you talk because you are part of a new family now, the family of God. Those old things have passed away, you've got a new life to live! Start living it.

There was a way my family lived. But God taught me how to do things differently! For that, I'm truly grateful. And that's why I want the world to know how good he is. I never accepted my kids getting upset and wanting to fight with their dad. That wasn't the way God taught us to live. When they were older, they came to me and said, "Mom, you were so right. You can't treat people the way they treat you, you have to treat them with love."

This is exactly what Jesus told us.

> ***"But to you who are listening I say: Love your enemies, do good to those who hate you, bless those who curse you, pray for those who mistreat you. If someone slaps you on one cheek, turn to them the other also. If someone takes your coat, do not withhold your shirt from them. Give to everyone who asks you, and if anyone takes what belongs to you, do not demand it back. Do to others as you would have them do to you.***
>
> ***If you love those who love you, what credit is that to you? Even sinners love those who love them. And if you do good to those who are good to you, what credit is that to you? Even sinners do that. And if you lend to those from whom you expect repayment, what credit is that to you? Even sinners lend to sinners, expecting to be repaid in full. But love your enemies, do good to them, and lend to them without expecting to get anything back. Then your reward will be great, and you will be children of the Most High, because he is kind to the ungrateful and wicked. Be merciful, just as your Father is merciful." Luke 6:27-36***

If God is in my life, and he is, there is no other way for me to live. This is the advice Jesus gave. As his followers, we must strive to live lives of love, not perfection. Perfection can never be obtained. We need to stop trying to make ourselves look good and start making God look good by the way we are living our lives.

Chapter 10

Dear Readers

As I wrote this book and took time to look back over my life, I realized there were many disappointing moments. Many hurts and pains that I didn't want to share with you. But what victory would there be if I were to keep silent. What the devil meant for evil in my life, God has turned around for good!

My dear reader, I am sharing all this for the glory of God. I'm putting myself on the altar as a sacrifice. Every hurt, every pain, may God use the awful in my life for His glory. May He use it to speak to your heart and allow you to understand that He is willing and able to do the same in your life—turn things around!

Jesus can heal everything you are going though right now; I'm a living witness of His miracle.

> ***"When Jesus had raised Himself up and saw no one but the woman, He said to her, "Woman, where are those accusers of yours? Has no one condemned you?"***
>
> ***She said, "No one, Lord."***

And Jesus said to her, "Neither do I condemn you; go and sin no more." John 8:10-11

When I look at the story of this woman that was accused, I see myself and I see the hope that God promises each of us. She was sentenced to death, but through the grace of God he spared her life. I know if God can spare her life, He is willing to do the same for us. No matter what we go through no matter how difficult life might be, we can always go back to our Heavenly Father. He'll be there to forgive us and accept us just like he did with this woman.

Jesus told her to go and sin no more.

"Therefore, if anyone is in Christ, he is a new creation; old things have passed away; behold, all things have become new." 2 Corinthians 5:17

We are brand new in Christ! This is what happens when we have an encounter with Him. We can see this with the Samaritan woman at the well. (John 4:1-26) When this woman encounters Jesus her life is changed forever. Jesus spoke to this woman while she was an outcast. He knew her situation intimately but He choose to seek her out, speak to her, and change her life. He wants the same for each of us.

After this encounter with Jesus, she went and told everyone who she had met and what He had done. Each day God is reaching out and doing the same for us. He is changing our situations. When He does, it is our responsibility and privilege to share with every one that we can about what he has done in our own lives.

God is in control over everything. He is bigger than our situations, our fears, our pain or even our sorrows. There is only one thing that he cannot do, fail! He is powerful enough to handle every situation that we face in our life please, do not fail to trust him and believe He is right there holding you hand. Keep believing that.

Jesus is the son of God. He died and rose again from the dead with all power and authority in his hand. Satan has no power or authority. No matter what we have been through in this world Jesus can fix it. He did so for many people in the Bible. If he did it for them, he will do it for us. Amen.

I just love it when Jesus says to Peter,

> ***"And I also say to you that you are Peter, and on this rock I will build My church, and the gates of Hades shall not prevail against it. And I will give you the keys of the kingdom of heaven, and whatever you bind on earth will be bound in heaven, and whatever you loose on earth will be loosed in heaven." Matthew 16:18-19***

Peter was a fisherman. But that was only his occupation. He was also was known for drinking, cursing, and fighting. He even denied Jesus Christ three times. Peter learned that we truly are weak and we must always rely on God rather than ourselves. Jesus didn't look at Peter's occupation or the things people knew him for. Instead, he looked at Peter's heart, He knew that Peter loved him.

God can use us too despite our failures. On the day of Pentecost, Peter preached to 3000 souls. God is so good! If he did it for Peter, he can do the same for you and me no matter what our shortcomings are.

God is the burden remover. The yoke destroyer. He is powerful and life-giving. He that began a good work in you will be faithful to complete it. He put each of us here for a purpose. I know that before Christ came into my life my heart was stony and cold; hardened by all the pain I had endured. When I asked Christ to come into my life, he gave me a heart of flesh. As he took away the hurt and pain, I began to open my heart more. As he came in, he broke down every wall I had constructed to keep myself safe from the world.

He is truly the almighty God and there is no God like him—north, south, east or west. He has touched my life and I am made whole. I didn't want to be that old woman that I used to be. I wanted to be the woman that he called me to be; a woman who could love and respect him, obey him and bring my children up in a Godly way.

> ***"And you, fathers, do not provoke your children to wrath, but bring them up in the training and admonition of the Lord." Ephesians 6:4***

Now that God had opened my eyes to the truth, I did not want my children to live the way I did. I thank God that he allowed me to be a better mom to my children and to teach them the fear and the love of Jesus. Today I want to love more, give more, be more patient, slow to speak but quick to hear, and more open to the spirit of God. I want to be a blessing for the Kingdom of God. And I encourage you dear readers to do the same.

God loves you. He has been waiting patiently for you to come so He can fix whatever you may be facing right now. He loves you and wants your soul to be healed. He is compassionate and long-suffering. Everything he does for you will work out for the good in your life and whatever the situation may be in your life God will be there for you.

I know that I am not rejected. My life is no longer in pieces but I am made whole through Christ. I'm never again going to seek anything that does not bring value to my life and the work of God. I will never again focus on the things in my past. I can see the sun coming up through those clouds, praise the Lord God Almighty! There is a reason for every season in our life. I thank you, Lord, for the seasons I have gone through which have made me stronger.

> ***"To everything there is a season, a time for every purpose under heaven." Ecclesiastes 3:1***

God, you've turned it all around for good. I want to thank you for being the light of my salvation. You have turned my sadness into joy unspeakable.

About the Author

Louise Rushing, is an Ordained Minister who has been teaching the word of God since 1998; a Phenomenal Speaker at many women's conferences across Washington. Author of *All Things Become New*, an inspirational book that has been an encouragement to so many. In her spare time, she loves to cook for the many people in her community, hosting dinners and special events sharing her culinary skills with love, Louise is a mother of two children and a grandmother to three beautiful grandsons and makes her home in SeaTac, Washington.